THE HOKEY POKEY OF POLITICS

by

Frank Romans

<u>**Other books by Frank Romans**</u>

**THE SIX SECRET TEACHINGS OF JIANG ZIYA:
a handbook for entrepreneurs**

UNDERSTANDING TAO and BEING GOOD

TAO OF PAPPY: on being DAD

<u>The Hokey Pokey</u>

You put your right foot in, you put your right foot out

You put your right foot in, and you shake it all about

You do the hokey pokey and you turn yourself around

That's what it's all about

You put your left foot in, you put your left foot out

You put your left foot in, and you shake it all about

You do the hokey pokey and you turn yourself around

That's what it's all about

You put your right hand in, you put your right hand out

You put your right hand in, and you shake it all about

You do the hokey pokey and you turn yourself around

That's what it's all about

You put your left hand in, you put your left hand out

You put your left hand in, and you shake it all about

You do the hokey pokey and you turn yourself around

That's what it's all about

You put your whole self in, you put your whole self out

You put your whole self in, and you shake it all about

You do the hokey pokey and you turn yourself around

That's what it's all about

For Patty, and for all of us.

Introduction

We have not been so divided as a people since the Civil War. There is a growing anger and resentment in our country. We are not divided just by race, but by class. We have become a country of haves and have nots. The greatness in our past came from the growth and expansion of a successful middle class. The middle class made America great, and we have sold our future to foreign governments and the greed of the wealthy few.

"The main problem in any democracy is that crowd-pleasers are generally brainless swine who can go out on a stage & whup their supporters into an orgiastic frenzy – then go back to the office & sell every one of the poor bastards down the tube for a nickel apiece." – Hunter S. Thompson, Fear and Loathing on the Campaign Trail '72

CONTENTS

Chapter One: Liberals

Why are some of us liberals? According to experts, liberals and conservatives do not just see things differently. They are different. The differences are not superficial and seem to run deep. It could just be part of our human nature to organize the world into right and left. But undoubtedly, liberals and conservatives have different personalities and view the world around them in different ways. The humor columnist Dave Barry described how Republicans think of Democrats as godless, unpatriotic, Volvo-driving, France-loving, elitist latte guzzlers. Liberals tend to highly value caring for people who are vulnerable and basic fairness, which for them means the equal sharing of resources. That is a noble idea, and to be fair, conservatives also care about those things. However, on fairness a conservative believes people get what they deserve based on their effort. A liberal's values strive to protect the rights of weaker members of society, and support diversity, different ideas, and ways of life.

Liberals believe in a government that protects individuals from being harmed by others. They believe government's most important job is to remove the barriers that prevent people from fully realizing their potential. These include poverty, disease, discrimination, and education. Liberalism has somewhat of a rocky relationship with democracy. Democracy gives the government authority through elections, while liberals are wary of the scope of a government's activity. When the majority elect the government, there is a danger of a tyranny of the majority. One could then argue that liberalism looks after the unpopular minorities.

From time to time, a political doctrine changes with the views of a generation. It is no different with liberals. Back in the nineteenth century liberals were basically the entrepreneurial and business middle class. There was a mistrust of governmental powers because of a fear of abuse of those powers. By the twentieth century the views had changed. There was support for an expansion of governmental power to restrict and regulate business to benefit laborers and consumers. The goal, however, was always to avoid the concentration of power that could threaten the individual; and a willingness to reform or add social institutions to fill those needs.

As liberals gained ground, conservatives argued their policies would be morally destructive, could ruin the economy, and be politically suicidal. The record shows things turned out much better. With increased social expenditures, labor and environmental regulation, and other reforms, the liberal capitalist democracies became more productive. Mortality and birth rates fell, per capita income rose, and the circle of prosperity expanded.

In today's modern world, it seems that liberalism is losing popularity. That is evident in America with a popular rebellion against liberal elites, who they see as out of touch with ordinary people. Those in the middle believe that liberals and their obsession with political correctness and minority rights, drove white voters to Donald Trump. Even Vladimir Putin has declared that liberalism is obsolete. So, is it wrong to demand that the government provide some degree of social and economic justice? Wasn't that the point of Roosevelt's New Deal?

Some writers blame liberalism as the cause of all our miseries. One could counter these principles were clearly expressed in our Bill of Rights and some of the first amendments to the Constitution. If we were to list the basic components of liberalism, it would have to include religious toleration, freedom of discussion, personal security, free elections, constitutional government, and economic progress.

Historically, most liberals have opposed, to some degree, the privileges of hereditary monopolies enjoyed by a few families. Some would have us believe that liberals are against any accumulation of wealth. That is not true. They accept the inequality of resources and know that it is the inevitable result from a good economy. While they remain concerned about poverty, and those at the bottom economically, they do not view wealth inequality as evil. They feel it is a moral obligation to provide a bottom level of subsistence which no one can fall below. They believe in the value of providing education for all, and a fair system of taxation. They have been somewhat antimilitaristic, believing in negotiations and rational debate over bloody conflicts.

For people in the middle, it seems liberal views today have become annoying with all the political correctness, and the cavalier racist label that gets slapped on whoever disagrees with them. Today, if a woman decides to wear a beautiful African or Asian styled dress, and she is not of that descent, she can be accused of "cultural appropriation."

Shouldn't it just be considered as a compliment on the beauty? It was not too long ago that gender identity disorder was considered a form of mental illness. Now one is considered a bigot if they have an issue with them using the ladies room. There are millions of people in the middle of these issues, and sensible conversations can be had, but many liberals are quick to criticize those who do not share their views, or may have been a little slower in keeping up.

Liberals have a strong platform since so many of the news media, entertainment industry, and college professors share their ideas. Certainly, there have been some cultural shifts in our society and these folks have a pulpit to espouse all these opinions and ideas. It may, in fact, have caused some Americans to reconsider their thoughts. Here is the problem: when you are on the big stage and self-righteously declare a huge segment of the country wrong and misguided, that reeks of superiority. "I am smarter and more enlightened than all of you." Self-righteousness can be wrong.

Liberals are reluctant to place any trust in the private sector. They are skeptical of conservative claims that the private sector could better manage or replace old government programs. Likewise, conservatives should not put so much blind trust in the private sector. Jeff Bezos of Amazon raked in $34,600,000,000 in two months of the COVID-19 pandemic. He touted his $100 million dollar donation to food banks but earned 346 times that amount in two months. Clearly, billionaire philanthropy is not the answer.

Politicians like to talk about the need for jobs, and we hear a lot about "good-paying" jobs vs. "low wage" jobs. This implies that lower wage jobs do not count. In times of crisis, such as a pandemic, I think we have learned that they are vitally important. Consider this: the real problem with a low paying job is the barrier to moving from welfare to work. If a lower paying job is available and one takes it, they can lose the medical benefits for their children. The conservative resistance to welfare really ignores many of the puzzle pieces that are at the height of a liberal's viewpoint, and the battle over universal healthcare is one that needs to be addressed and resolved. Coming to grips with poverty in America is something conservatives can learn from liberals.

To really eradicate poverty, we should consider UBI. Universal Basic Income, or UBI, is an idea that has been ridiculed and rejected in America. That thinking may be wrong, and the 2020 pandemic helps to illustrate the point. UBI in normal times is the floor that paychecks add to. Instead of the citizenry having to navigate all those unemployment bureaucracies, with UBI in place we could have simply agreed to temporarily increase the amount until the crisis is over. This idea of a basic income guarantee should move to the forefront of political discussions. If we really care about our populace and eradicating poverty, this is an idea with merit, and perhaps the time has come to consider it.

Currently, as of this writing, we are still in the middle of a global pandemic of the COVID-19 virus. It is interesting that Republicans and Democrats view this virus so differently. In May 2020, a research survey found that only 39 percent of Republicans had serious concerns about it, while 97 percent of Democrats said they had serious concerns. Furthermore, Republican governors have been very reluctant to impose any restrictions in their states. That is not to say that a conservative values their constituents any less than a liberal, but where liberals have a core belief in protecting the people over other considerations, conservatives have a higher concern over the infringement on civil liberties. It is concerning to see the abandonment of civil liberties in the enthusiasm to protect the public. It appears we may be dealing with this virus for a while and allowing certain liberties to be removed is problematic. Hopefully, those in power will find some balance in their decisions, and the American people will unify and get behind those decisions.

A problem has emerged within liberalism. The belief that only their views can be the foundation for a fair and just society, and anything else is illicit. Further, the view that old boundaries and limits must be removed does require a bit of social engineering.

In a liberal's ideal society there is room for all beliefs, no matter how bizarre. All have the space to fulfill their desires, and all peacefully coexist. The reality is that it can never be completely achieved, and most liberals agree. However, they argue we should be striving towards that utopian goal. The problem is removing those old limits. This requires removing from those who may have been privileged to grant to those who have been disadvantaged.

On practically every college campus today, there is an Office of Diversity and Inclusion, fully staffed with campus bureaucrats. They are there to combat mankind's history of discrimination by whites against blacks, men against women, Europeans against non-Europeans, sexism, racism, homophobia, and any other ism or phobia you can think of. All these forces must be monitored and eliminated. The danger with liberalism is the movement toward pluralism. This rigid ideology condemns all who disagree as moral criminals. Does this remind anyone of what Orwell called thought crimes? Must we be in fear of using the wrong pronoun? Must we silence all with a differing view who would dare to speak at a university?

Former President Obama referred to inequality as "the defining issue of our time." He was right then, and it is true now. The question is, what do we do about it?

Liberals talk about the need to raise taxes on the wealthy, and that may be a good idea. Even some billionaires have indicated they should probably pay more in taxes. That is not the complete solution that is needed. The United States is a wealthy country, and although supply-side conservatives would disagree, we can afford to tax the wealthiest 1% and corporations more without slowing economic growth. It has puzzled me how during a pandemic we could quickly heed the cries for help from business, and muster the government funded help. As soon as the narrative shifts to boosted unemployment or stimulus payments to Americans, there is an affordability crisis. The same goes for discussions on social security, universal healthcare, and on and on. The public could perceive this attitude to mean that many political figures dislike us, and feel we are undeserving of any help.

One of the principal reasons for such difficulty with tax increases on the wealthy is the pain of loss for those affected. The 1% group can easily handle an increase, as well as large corporations. But any such increases probably need to also impact the six figure income folks, who are not in that 1% but are big earners, the so-called "dream hoarders." These individuals have an aversion to any losses, and the power and resources to mobilize and protect what they have. That is a difficult political challenge to overcome as the word "taxes" is a dirty word in America.

No one would dispute that the political climate today is highly partisan. It seems compromise is an impossibility, and all believe their opinion represents fact. When you consider the common stereotypes about liberals and conservatives, it makes sense. Liberals are viewed as bleeding hearts and conservatives are cold-hearted. Conservatives want limited government and cuts to social programs that help the unfortunate. Liberals do not mind paying a little more in taxes to help those in need.

There was an interesting study by researchers in Belgium, where a group of students took a series of emotional understanding tests. The results were unanimous. They found that those who scored lower on the emotional ability tests also scored higher on "measures of right-wing authoritarianism and social dominance orientation." People within that disposition set are more willing to subject themselves to authority figures (political, police, religious leaders) and are more hostile to those outside of their groups. This type of person is attracted to authoritarian leaders like Donald Trump.

If you are into studies and polls, a national poll showed most Americans lean to the left. Americans are upset about the ever-growing inequality, big business influence, and declining living standards. With so much focus on bigotry and divisions, the fact that most of us have some liberal views gets hidden. Most Americans are concerned that our government has been captured by the powerful and wealthy. Most would support some governmental involvement to address problems like climate change and health care.

Jonathan Haidt, from the University of Virginia, has identified five foundational moral impulses. They are:

- Harm/Care. It is wrong to hurt people; it is good to relieve suffering.
- Fairness/Reciprocity. Justice and fairness are good; people have certain rights that need to be upheld in social interactions.
- In-Group Loyalty. People should be true to their group and be wary of threats from the outside. Allegiance, loyalty, and patriotism are virtues; betrayal is bad.
- Authority/Respect. People should respect social hierarchy; social order is necessary for human life.
- Purity/Sanctity. The body and certain aspects of life are sacred. Cleanliness and health, as well as their derivatives of chastity and piety, are all good. Pollution,

contamination, and the associated character traits of lust and greed are all bad.

His research concludes that liberals feel strongly about the first two, but not so much about the other three. Conservatives, on the other hand, feel strongly about loyalty, authority, and purity. They accept the importance of harm prevention and fairness, but not so strongly as liberals.

When you read about, or study TAO, one learns about the importance of balance and opposing principles. Liberalism and conservatism are those opposing principles and will work well if in balance.

Haidt says, and I think rightfully so, that if liberals ran the whole world it would fall apart. But if conservatives ran the whole world, it would be so restrictive and uncreative, that it too would be very unpleasant.

The liberal world view is rather optimistic. They see the world as amiable and benign. They see government as the tool of a democracy to solve problems and improve the well-being of the people. Conservatives are more pessimistic about the world. They see the world as a challenging place, where other countries are eager to take advantage over us. They believe in taking strong measures to counter potential threats. These differing views of the world explain their respective stance on so many of the issues of the day.

The First Amendment of the United States Constitution reads: "Congress shall make no law respecting an establishment of religion, or prohibiting the free exercise thereof; or abridging the freedom of speech, or of the press; or the right of the people peaceably to assemble, and to petition the government for a redress of grievances." Since they perceive the world as less threatening, liberals tend to be less religious than conservatives. Additionally, they rely on science and education as the best way to solve problems. Conservatives are mostly religious because religious rituals promote feelings of safety in what they view as a dangerous world.

The Second Amendment of the United States Constitution reads: "A well-regulated Militia, being necessary to the security of a Free State, the right of the people to keep and bear Arms, shall not be infringed." Such language has created considerable debate regarding the Amendment's intended scope. Liberals feel that protection of citizens against crime is better left to police, and that armed citizens are a threat to those around them. Conservatives are pro-gun because they want to be able to defend themselves against criminal threats of any type.

The Fourteenth Amendment of the United States Constitution addresses many aspects of citizenship and the rights of citizens. It was ratified in 1868 and granted citizenship to all persons born or naturalized in the United States, including former slaves. It guaranteed all citizens equal protection of the laws. Liberals do not see foreigners or racial and ethnic minorities as a threat. Conservatives have tended to view them as potential threats and have been less welcoming.

Liberals feel excessive military buildups and warfare drain too much capital from social programs, whereas conservatives favor a strong military and aggressive foreign policy. Liberals are OK with taxes, so long as the money is being used for the well-being of the people. They believe government should reflect the will of the people. Except for military defense, conservatives do not want any governmental intrusions into their lives and are resistant to having their wealth impacted through taxation.

Conservatives are very pro-Family and feel that having a strong family around them is the best possible defense against any threat, perceived or real. A liberal does not see familial ties as that much of a protection. They will support welfare programs for the poor and feel that is the best way to reduce child poverty, crime, and social problems. On the other hand, conservatives feel this encourages dependency and stifles incentive.

Liberals are very suspicious of the wealthy. Right or wrong, they tend to believe much of their wealth was either inherited or obtained by unscrupulous methods, undermining social trust. Conservatives seem to admire the wealthy and see them as champions of hard work, fulfilling their obligations to provide for their families in a difficult world.

Another problem with liberals is they can sometimes be viewed as snobs. Since they call the Democratic Party home, the Democratic Party is thus filled with snobs. The definition of the liberal elite is a group of people with education, money, and other advantages, often living in cities, who have liberal political views, and are seen as not understanding the problems and the views of ordinary people. In a 2016 campaign speech, Hillary Clinton referred to half of Trump's supporters as a "Basket of Deplorables". She later admitted that may have been one of the factors in her loss to Donald Trump. In Oliver Stone's "Nixon" there is a scene where Nixon stands in front of a picture of Kennedy, and says, "When they look at you, they see what they want to be. When they look at me, they see what they are." He, of course, is referring to the young, handsome, rich, Harvard-educated Kennedy vs. himself, who grew up in a poor family in Southern California.

Although liberalism has lost some ground to conservatives, the future seems bright for liberal ideas. If we look at where the generational divides are, it gives us a picture of where we are likely heading. Millenials have moved into their twenties and thirties, and a new generation is coming into focus. Generation Z, diverse and set to become the most educated yet, is moving toward adulthood. This will be interesting to observe.

On most issues, Generation Z's views are the same as those of millennials. These views differ from the older generations and there are clues for the future. According to PEW Research Center, only about 30% approve of Trump as President. Most of them feel government should do more to solve social problems and agree that minorities are treated unfairly. They think racial and ethnic diversity is good for society and have positive views of inter-racial and same-sex marriages. This younger, diverse population will soon begin flexing its political muscle, and that will raise our national consciousness on many progressive issues. This will contrast with the aging baby boomer population, who have resisted these ideas. It has been suggested that the politicians who decide matters on climate change will be dead by the time the proverbial shit hits the fan. The younger crowd feel since it is them who will have to deal with it, they should have a say. Some have also suggested that Brexit would not have happened if 16-17 years old voting were allowed.

Do you see where this is going? The average age of Congress has been steadily increasing since the 1980's. And how old are the current presidential candidates? The federal bureaucracy is even older than the general U.S. work force. Evidently, those generous defined-benefit pensions for civil-servant boomers keep them on the job longer. Our leaders and our government are getting old, and we are ruled by the geezer class. As younger people begin to enter the ranks, greater diversity is coming. Personally, I am ready to hand them the reigns, with a hope they will do and be better.

The following is attributed to Ron Howard, who got it from the supposed source, Lori Gallagher Witt. I am including it here because in many ways, it accurately reflects my own views. I am a sort of liberal, but that does not mean what a lot of you apparently think it does. Let's break it down, shall we? Because quite frankly, I am getting a little tired of being told what I believe and what I stand for. Spoiler alert: not every liberal is the same, although the majority that I know think along roughly these same lines.

1. I believe a country should take care of its weakest members. A country cannot call itself civilized when its children, disabled, sick, and elderly are neglected. PERIOD.

2. I believe healthcare is a right, not a privilege. Somehow that is interpreted as "I believe Obamacare is the end-all, be-all." This is not the case. I am fully aware that the ACA has problems, that a national healthcare system would require everyone to chip in, and that it is impossible to create one that is devoid of flaws, but I have yet to hear an argument against it that makes "let people die because they can't afford healthcare" a better alternative. I believe healthcare should be far cheaper than it is, and that everyone should have access to it. And no, I am not opposed to paying higher taxes in the name of making that happen.

3. I believe education should be affordable. It doesn't necessarily have to be free (though it works in other countries so I am mystified as to why it can't work in the U.S.), but at the end of the day, there is no excuse for students graduating college saddled with five or six figure debt. I also believe we should stop

glorifying a college degree over trade schools.

4. I don't believe your money should be taken from you and given to people who do not want to work. I have literally never encountered anyone who believes this. Ever. I just have a massive moral problem with a society where a handful of people can possess the majority of the wealth while there are people literally starving to death, freezing to death, or dying because they can't afford to go to the doctor. Fair wages, lower housing costs, universal healthcare, affordable education, and the wealthy paying their share would go a long way toward alleviating this. I do not think believing this way makes me a communist.

5. I do not throw around "I am willing to pay higher taxes" lightly. If I am suggesting something that involves paying more, it is because I am fine with paying my share, as long as it is actually going to something besides lining corporate pockets or

bombing other countries, while Americans die without healthcare.

6. I believe companies should be required to pay their employees a decent, livable wage. Somehow this gets interpreted as me wanting burger flippers to be able to afford a penthouse apartment and a Mercedes. What it means is that no one should have to work two or three full-time jobs just to keep their head above water. Restaurant workers should not have to rely on tips, multibillion-dollar companies should not have employees on food stamps, workers shouldn't have to work themselves into the ground just to barely make ends meet, and minimum wage should be enough for someone to work 40 hours and live.

7. I am not anti-Christian. I have no desire to stop Christians from being Christians, to close churches, to ban the Bible, to forbid prayer in school, etc. (By the way, prayer in school is NOT illegal; *compulsory* prayer in school is, and should be, illegal). When I get angry that a politician is trying

to legislate Scripture into law, I'm not offended by Christianity; I'm offended by their attempt to force me to live by their religion's rules. I am equally upset at the thought of Muslims trying to impose Sharia law. Be a Christian. Be a Muslim. Do your thing. Just do not try to force your beliefs on me or mine.

8. I do not believe LGBT people should have more rights than you. I just believe they should have the SAME rights as you.

9. I do not believe illegal immigrants should come to America and have the world at their feet, especially since that is not true. I do not know where this narrative comes from, but here are the facts. Undocumented immigrants are ineligible for all those programs they are supposed to be abusing, and if they are "stealing your job" it is because your employer is hiring illegally. I believe there are far more humane ways to handle undocumented immigration than our current practices. (i.e., detaining

children, splitting up families, ending DACA, etc.).

10. I do not believe the government should regulate everything, but since greed is such a driving force in our country, we need regulations to prevent cutting corners, environmental destruction, tainted food/water, unsafe materials in consumable goods or medical equipment, etc. It is not that I want the government's hands in everything; I just don't trust the people whose primary goal is making money to be the ones to ensure that their products, practices etc. are actually safe. Is the government devoid of shadiness? Of course not. But with those regulations in place, consumers have recourse if they are harmed, and companies are liable for medical bills, environmental cleanup, etc. Just kind of seems like common sense when the alternative to government regulation is letting companies bring their bottom line into the equation.

11. I believe our current administration may be leaning toward fascism. I have spent too many years reading and learning about the Third Reich to miss the similarities. Not because any administration I dislike must be Nazis, but because things today are mirroring authoritarian and fascist regimes of the past.

12. I believe the systemic racism and misogyny in our society is much worse than many people think, and desperately needs to be addressed. Which means those with privilege---white, straight, male, economic, etc.---need to start listening, even if you do not like what you are hearing, so we can start dismantling everything that is causing people to be marginalized.

13. I am not interested in coming after your blessed guns, nor is anyone serving in government. What I am interested in is the enforcement of present laws and enacting new, common sense gun regulations.

14. I believe in a certain level of so-called political correctness. I prefer to think it is social politeness. If I call you Chuck and you say you prefer to be called Charles, I will call you Charles. It's the polite thing to do. Not because everyone is a delicate snowflake, but because as Maya Angelou put it, when we know better, we do better. When someone tells you that a term or phrase is more accurate/less hurtful than the one you are using, you now know better. So why not do better? How does it hurt you to not hurt another person?

15. I believe in funding sustainable energy, including offering education to people currently working in coal or oil so they can change jobs. There are too many sustainable options available for us to continue with coal and oil. Surely, we can figure this out.

16. I believe that women should not be treated as a separate class of human. They should be paid the same as men

who do the same work, should have the same rights as men, and should be free from abuse. Why on earth shouldn't they be?

I think that about covers it. Bottom line is I'm a liberal because I think we should take care of each other. That doesn't mean you should work 80 hours a week so your lazy neighbor can get all your money. It just means I don't believe there is any scenario in which preventable suffering is an acceptable outcome as long as money is saved.

Chapter Two: Conservatives

Why are some of us conservatives? In the history of the United States, there are those who lean conservative and those who lean liberal no matter their political party. Conservatives have generally sought to conserve the status quo, seemingly in favor of the wealthy and ruling class, as well as the business community. Liberals have typically advocated for change to benefit everyone, especially the disadvantaged and minorities. Conservatives, on the other hand, are resistant to any quick changes and mistrust what they view as an attempt by liberals to remake society.

The philosophical founder of this modern conservatism is Edmund Burke. As a member of parliament with the WHIG party, he was a supporter of the American colonies and their complaints about taxation but opposed the attempt to achieve independence. He felt the French Revolution was destroying the fabric of good society, which led to him becoming a conservative leader. According to Burke, when the French overthrew their monarchy, they abandoned their past, their history, and all social and political conventions of a civilized society. He did not want to see that repeated.

The central tenets of conservatism include tradition, organic society, hierarchy, authority, and property rights. For a conservative, organic society means local, rural, and traditional rather than cosmopolitan, urban, and mobile. In America, conservatism has been chiefly associated with the Republican Party, and defends against modernist culture and secularism. For example, they support school prayer and oppose abortion and homosexuality.

Conservatives have a desire to preserve the political philosophy and rules of government spelled out in our Declaration of Independence and U.S. Constitution. While they may agree that the application of our laws should adapt as society changes and modernizes, they do not agree with some progressives who view the Constitution as a "living document."

"I will not attempt to discover whether legislation is 'needed' before I have first determined whether it is constitutionally permissible." – Sen. Barry Goldwater

Today, many conservatives believe that the Constitution does not explicitly delegate powers to the federal government, and that issues should be left to the states.

In addition to the interest in preserving governmental traditions from our history, there is a strong belief in preserving and promoting morality as it is articulated in the Bible. Religion and politics make uneasy bedfellows. An interesting study out of Stanford University found there is a different Jesus in the minds of liberal and conservative Christians. The Republican Jesus tended to be against wealth redistribution, illegal immigrants, abortion, and same-sex marriage; whereas the Democratic Jesus had far more liberal opinions. Politicians and preachers, with their fellow believers, tend to emphasize the aspects of Christianity that prove their point. Conservatives tout the Old Testament with its homophobic rhetoric and eye for an eye morality, and liberals quote the New Testament where Jesus was sympathetic to the poor and meek.

Most evangelical Christians today believe there is a moral decline in our country because too many laws legislating morality have been struck down. There is an overused expression, "you can't legislate morality." That means we should not try to make laws based on religious beliefs. It seems to me that what people are wanting to legislate are social customs that have changed and do not coincide with their beliefs or religion. There is a frustration with the difficulty of convincing others to believe as you believe, and so often political force has been used to ensure compliance.

Conservatives believe in a free market economy, where prices are set through the law of supply and demand, with limited governmental intervention. The United States is by far the world's premier free market economy, although the reality is that we are both a free market and a command economy. America has successfully blended the best of both. When we think of a command economy, what comes to mind is all those communist regimes, or perhaps some monarchies. Even these countries are adopting some free market principles to compete in the global economy. The truth is that China (yes, China) does capitalism better than most. The government, though still communist, tolerates entrepreneurship because they recognize they must, to compete. And look how successful they have become. Hong Kong has been touted as the world's freest economy. Singapore too, has been a strong free market economy.

Economists will forever debate a solution to the deficit problem however, we have learned that strategic spending creates jobs, increases production, and reduces overall expenses. Here is an interesting fact to consider: The Political Economy Research Institute found that $1 billion in military spending added 11,200 jobs, while $1 billion in education spending created 26,700 jobs. It would seem how to spend money to stimulate our free market is abundantly clear.

We can debate about the winners and losers of free market economies, and I believe there is a common viewpoint that capitalism rewards winners because they have been industrious, efficient, prudent, frugal, and disciplined. Conversely, that same viewpoint is that the losers are lazy, inefficient, or negligent. This thinking is wrong. What about when the losers are children, the disabled, or the elderly? Here are some painful facts:

- The U.S.A. has the highest overall poverty rate of any industrialized country.
- The once-thriving middle class is being squeezed into extinction.

- Trickle-down theories have not and do not work. After all these years, we have proven it.

If conservatives continue to ignore these problems, there will be a reckoning. We are now living in the most polarized country since just before the Civil War, and the left and right need to find compromise.

"America is a shining city upon a hill whose beacon light guides freedom-loving people everywhere." – President Ronald Reagan

Conservatives strongly believe in American exceptionalism, and feel the United States is the rightful leader of the free world. Few could dispute that America is exceptional. It has created the most prosperous nation in history, and our democratic principles inspire all those who desire to be free. We were founded on a creed of liberty and the protection of rights. We fought a Civil War to grant these rights to African-Americans. Our role as a world leader was based on this creed and no other country on earth could perform as we have. Even after World Wars we never occupied other countries. We rebuilt and brought in democracy. No other country, even if rich and militarily powerful, could be trusted to do this.

Some conservatives have believed in exporting our exceptionalism and our form of democracy through forceful means to the rest of the world. The results of this are mixed. We did it in Germany and Japan, but what about Cuba and Vietnam? Residents of these countries do not have the historical background that we do. We had a habit of self-governance and forming associations to allow for problem solving. In his "Democracy in America," Alexis de Tocqueville suggested that it was a major factor of why democracy worked in America. That would explain the chaos during the Iraq reconstruction, and what was estimated to cost $100 billion to $200 billion, and has now become $2 trillion. Iraqis do not share that habit of cooperation and self-governance.

If societies do not have the historical reference from their past and are unstable, perhaps a better way is through democratic promotion assistance. We could provide training for leadership, networking among activists and entrepreneurs, and technical training. Coupled with financial assistance these could over time achieve the goal of exporting democracy without acting militarily. I suggest it would be worth the effort. Conservatives understand we must protect America, and promoting democracy is linked closely to that goal. We should exercise caution that we do not make things worse in that pursuit.

There is much discussion about rebuilding our infrastructure, especially just before an election. I have been hearing about this most of my adult life, though little is done no matter which party is in office. Conservatives are fond of grand projects to advance our national greatness and create that multitude of good paying jobs, yet as our roads and bridges collapse around us, nothing gets done. President Trump promised to induce $1 trillion of public and private investment in infrastructure over a decade. Democrats had their own $1 trillion plan. Sadly, these fade away until the next election cycle when we start up the arguments again. The problem compounds when state and local governments delay funding projects hoping for federal funds.

Conservatives are correct to lobby for megaprojects. They can be economically transformative both at home and abroad. Just consider projects like the Panama Canal. Think about the opportunities around the world where countries need infrastructure. It has been estimated that the world needs to spend around $57 trillion by 2030. What a huge opportunity!

Although Democrats began flirting with the localist mantra and state rights during the Obama years, it seems to be forgotten since they won back the House and smell blood for 2020. Now there seems to be a desire to centralize even more power in Washington. This could cost them in elections because Americans tend to favor localism for decisions that affect them. Supporting states' rights and localism has long been the conservative position. But the truth is both Republican and Democratic parties have at times abandoned localism.

We have witnessed failures over centralized control on everything from housing and education to economic opportunity initiatives. Local citizens acting in the interest of their communities makes sense. What works in New York may not work in Texas. The problem with shifting the great number of decisions to the community level lies with protecting individual freedoms and rights. Our past from not so long ago has examples of local/state governments clashing with federal law. We are a nation of differences. We have different ethnicities, lifestyle preferences, and cultural beliefs. Some argue that the federal government should stay out of their business. That is a solid conservative opinion. Yet at the same time, they argue against the right of a local government elsewhere, such as with sanctuary cities. Progressives may view the states' rights argument as code for white supremacy. Perhaps the best solution is to let the states do what they want, so long as it is not breaking federal law or violating the Constitution. Their own electorate will hold them accountable and then we can lessen the arguments over moral issues. It may be a utopian view but also may be the only workable solution compared to what we have now.

There is a belief among conservatives that America should not intervene in the affairs of other nations unless it is to defend ourselves. Conservatives believe that no country has the capability to solve all the world's problems. They want to show restraint and leave other countries alone.

Today's conservative appears to have left this brand of conservatism behind. They vote for ever-increasing defense budgets, maintaining countless bases around the world, and support ongoing wars. There is a certain irony in their support of reducing our government's role in American lives, while increasing it abroad. It does not escape me that there is also irony in liberal American politician's views that we know best and need to export our "best" around the world. A true conservative would find this ridiculous, but it does explain the bipartisan efforts to intervene around the globe. These nation building projects are not only costly in money and lives but are radical as well.

There is a certain nostalgia for the way it used to be among conservatives. They have a view of the world as depicted by the art of Norman Rockwell and yearn for the return of those simpler times of Mom, home, apple pie, and the American way. Donald Trump perfectly exploited this with his "Make America Great Again" campaign. This played well with older white males and propelled him into the presidency. The nostalgia for the 1950's and 1960's may not be shared by a black person or a woman. I would remind those with these nostalgic yearnings that in those days corporate tax rates were higher and labor unions controlled a large share of the workforce.

Americans used to live comfortably in suburban towns, secure in their employment with the same company. They belonged to unions and had neighborhood solidarity, where their kids went to the same schools and churches, they owned their homes and frequented the same establishments. Today, much of that has been stripped away and there is a resentment of liberal policies that they feel are unfairly subsidizing immigrants and minorities. As stated earlier, they view liberals in the cities as "elites" who don't care about them and are out of touch with reality. Conservative politics has stepped in to fill the void and we have seen the rise of hardline, far right views; in supporting traditional families, gun ownership for protection, advocacy for church and religion, plus flag and nation. These social conservatives want laws that uphold their traditional values, such as opposition to same sex marriage, abortion, and a tough stand on law and order issues. Conservatives hold the view that liberalism, for all its good intentions of multiculturalism, identity politics, affirmative action, welfare, and social policies, will never produce the desired results. They believe history is on their side, and if we will just look at the evidence from governments around our world, we should see it too. They see liberal democracy as leading to socialism, which leads to control in the hands of a dictator. No one seeks that outcome, but their belief is liberal policies always bring that result in the end.

Does anyone remember President Reagan's promise to "get the government off the backs of the great American people?" Conservatives believe it is their natural right to be left alone by the government. They do not want the federal government intruding on what they see as the local or state's turf and support the concept of Federalism. Conflicts between national and state governments are common and was one of the factors that led to our Civil War. Today's federal government has amassed a great deal of power. This has led to overregulation and a redundant bureaucracy. Republicans and conservatives are right to voice concern over any imbalance between federal and state/local matters. Most of us are all over the map on these issues, but the hallmarks of the conservative position are controlled spending, low taxes, and a balanced budget.

Although these positions sound good on paper, when you look at decreasing our debt the political will dissolves quickly. To reduce our debt requires cutting spending. Congress fears that drastically cutting spending will slow economic growth. In 2010 the Simpson-Bowles deficit reduction plan offered ways to resolve the national debt. The bipartisan report was never adopted by Congress.

Opponents were unwilling to touch social security, medicare, or defense spending, because it was too politically difficult. In America, cuts to programs or added taxes will not get you reelected.

When it comes to foreign policy, conservatives have typically been realists and believed that nations are always motivated by self-interest. To our detriment, for the past twenty- five or so years a neoconservative approach has dominated. Hindsight now allows us to see that the past quarter century was a failure. We are overdue for conversations about these failures in the Iraq war, the nation building attempt in Afghanistan, the intervention in Libya, and the effort to create a democratic opposition in Syria. A return to a core tenet of conservatism, a hands-off approach to foreign policy is needed. The events and actions from our most recent past have resulted in greater international tensions and a course correction is needed.

A true conservative is conscious of man's fallibility and realizes they cannot know everything and are open to expanding their knowledge through experiences and evidence from other people. They understand the value of a healthy skepticism while they gather facts and believe in the virtue of humility. I share many of their views along with my liberal views, and I suspect most of you do as well.

Chapter Three: Independents & Libertarians

Independents

Why are some of us Independents? An independent voter does not align themselves with a political party. They vote for candidates of either party based on issues thus are often referred to as swing votes.

A recent Pew Research Center report took a detailed look at the large share of Americans who identify as independents. They found that a whopping 38% of U.S. adults claim to be independents, but most lean toward one of the two major parties. So, what is important to an independent? Interestingly, the recent impeachment discussions had them split evenly, with a slight edge favoring impeachment. They overwhelmingly reject the notion of separating immigrant children from their parents at the border and agree with Democrats. When it comes to a gun ban, the support is solidly in the Republican camp, with eighty percent of them rejecting a total ban on guns. This pattern continues right on down the line on other hot-button issues, so in an election either party could find independents swinging their way if they have the right package.

Some argue that independent votes could make up as high as 45% of us. But for sure, independents share the view that the two major political parties are failing us and are putting their own interests ahead of the country and the American people. Most independents care deeply about the process of elections. They argue against the pitfalls they see in the process; the closed primaries that lock out millions of voters, the controlled presidential debates, the convention delegate selection rules, the electoral college, and on and on. It would be hard to disagree with the unfairness of it all. The two predominant parties tightly control this process for a reason and the reason should be obvious.

As the ranks of independents have grown, there has been a desire for an alternative. We saw the rise of campaigns from the likes of Ross Perot, Lenora Fulani, Ron Paul, and Ralph Nader. The major parties attacked these outsiders relentlessly and thumbed their noses at a large swath of voters.

There have been third party victories in Senate races from time to time, and of course, one of the more notable Senators is Bernie Sanders (VT). Senator Angus King (ME) has served since 2013 and Senator Sanders since 2007.

Here is the problem with our current system. There is low competition because both parties rigged the rules to protect their power. They draw their own district lines and discriminate against third parties. That makes the primary the only election that matters in their "safe" districts. They keep too many obstacles in the way of voters casting a ballot and are rewarded with low participation in primaries and a shut out of the independents. With their party primaries dominated by party activists and special interest groups, politicians can escape any accountability to their constituency. How do you make sure politicians listen to ALL their constituents? Simple: by giving all their constituents a voice in their election through open and nonpartisan primaries.

A solution to the gerrymandering is to remove the power of districting from politicians and put it in the hands of Independent Redistricting Commissions.

Another problem is the fear voters have in supporting independent or third-party candidates. They fear their vote will be wasted, could spoil the election, and cause their least favorite candidate to be elected. There has been a solution proposed to this with Ranked Choice Voting. Voting this way would end that spoiler effect by allowing voters to rank their candidates according to preference, ensuring a majority winner. This could provide another positive benefit by encouraging more civility in our elections. The candidates could appeal to their opponent's supporters for second place votes.

Facts:

- Maine uses Ranked Choice Voting for state elections.
- Five states use Ranked Choice Voting for overseas and military voters.
- Twenty municipalities either use or have approved Ranked Choice Voting.
- Democratic primary contests in Nevada, Alaska, Wyoming, Kansas, and Hawaii that used RCV in their primaries, broke turnout records in every state.

There is something wrong about voting for a candidate that does not back policies you support or engages in conduct you find inappropriate. That is why our current system is so flawed. The wide range of political opinions is far too diverse to be isolated into two groups that essentially seem the same. There may be a certain moral satisfaction that comes with declaring as an independent but in a way, it also is a surrender. Voting for third-party candidates is today, still mostly a symbolic gesture. When candidate Trump defeated Hillary Clinton, Jill Stein was clearly a spoiler in Michigan and Wisconsin. If not for Stein, those electoral votes would have likely gone to Clinton.

There is a joke that independents are merely Democrats and Republicans in sheep's clothing. For myself, I started out Republican but found myself sometimes voting for the Democrat or Independent. Over time, I changed my registration to Independent and became annoyed with closed primaries, so switched back to Republican. My views are generally for some of both, not either/or. My circle may be small, but I believe most Americans agree with some things on one side and some on the other. We are the people in the middle.

Libertarians

What does it mean to be a Libertarian? Why are some of us libertarians?

According to definition: Libertarians seek to maximize political freedom and autonomy, emphasizing individualism, freedom of choice, and voluntary association. They share a skepticism of authority and state power, but they diverge on the scope of their opposition to existing economic and political systems.

That is a mouthful of definition. The libertarian perspective is that peace, prosperity, and social harmony is fostered by as much liberty as possible and as little government as necessary. They have a long tradition of supporting and contributing to movements that changed history. Some of these are abolition, women's suffrage, and the civil rights movement.

Where liberals favor governmental actions to promote equality, and conservatives favor it to keep order, libertarians do not want any action from the government for equality or order. They believe people have the right to live as they wish so long as they do not infringe on the rights of others.

There are many prominent figures from our past that have supported libertarian thoughts and ideas. Among these are James Madison, Thomas Jefferson, and of course, the well-known author, Ayn Rand.

Libertarians are neither liberal nor conservative. They do advocate for high degrees of personal and economic liberty. On economic matters they believe in lowering and eliminating taxes, slashing regulation of business, and support charitable rather than government welfare. They oppose any law that seeks to control one's personal choices, for example the use of marijuana. They believe individuals have the right to decide what they consume. Libertarians favor repealing laws that punish for so-called victimless crimes such as gambling, recreational drug use, and consensual sexual services or prostitution. They also oppose the death penalty.

Libertarians want to repeal the income tax and abolish the IRS. They support any removal of taxation and believe public services should be funded voluntarily to the extent that is possible. Additionally, they want a balanced budget amendment to the U.S. Constitution.

They are against defined-benefit pensions in government employment (they are already gone for the private sector). Libertarians want a completely free market and oppose all forms of subsidies and bailouts.

Here is a big one. They would do away with Social Security and transition to a private voluntary system.

Wow, that is a bundle of anti-government involvement. You will have to decide if you agree with any of it, and I feel compelled to mention this here. Regarding the whole balanced budget amendment and eliminating spending ideas of libertarians, conservatives, and some liberals too; I have a suggestion. It is this: Read and educate yourselves on MMT (Modern Monetary Theory) by obtaining Stephanie Kelton's book, *The Deficit Myth*. It will enlighten you.

Chapter Four: Talk Radio & Television

The rise of talk radio has been surging for years, most predominantly conservative talk radio. Obviously, the success of syndicated hosts like Rush Limbaugh, Glenn Beck, and Mark Levin proves there is a high demand for these shows, but if we dig a bit deeper we will find industry changes that helped contribute to their growth. Deregulation and technology played a part. Rather than local players, media giants took over. Technology changed the way we listen to music and music programming became less profitable.

In the late 1980's, AM radio was losing advertising dollars to FM stations because music sounded better there. The AM stations were looking for something new, and most would agree they found their answer in a top-40 disc-jockey, Rush Limbaugh. On August 1, 1988 he debuted nationally, was a big success, and radio executives began filling their time slots with more conservative hosts.

At first, it seemed the goal was simply to entertain with humorous political parodies and some outrageous comedy. But by the mid-1990's the

GOP had begun utilizing them to push agendas and win elections. To keep their audiences, the hosts grew more extreme and the tail (talk radio) began to wag the dog (GOP). Today, after several decades of conservative talk radio, we have politicians sounding more like talk show hosts. President Trump regularly mentions Rush Limbaugh and Sean Hannity, and in a surprise move during a State of the Union address, awarded Limbaugh the Medal of Freedom. It is clear these radio hosts have amassed a great deal of power.

Though there are many conservative talk stations, few liberal alternatives exist. It would seem the public does not want that. Additionally, the Democratic party has not been supportive. It may be that Democrats view this as a right-wing thing and do not see any value. It has also been suggested that their supporters get information in other ways. Whatever the reason, the airwaves are dominated by their conservative rivals.

One wonders if talk radio's power makes it difficult for elected officials to govern. If a Republican must worry about the wrath of a radio host, can they be as effective? Remember, these people spend hours every day with an audience that practically views them as family and will react when the host tells them something is wrong. When political thought is influenced by a host that has no standard of credibility, it could be considered demagogic or even unethical. These programs utilize call screening, oversimplification with half-truths, and opinions with no documentation. Whether fortunate or unfortunate, tens of millions get their information from talk radio. Certainly, there are good and bad radio hosts, but Rush Limbaugh, the most popular of them all, regularly misinforms his audience with inaccurate facts. Today, since transcripts of the programs exist online, it is simple to fact-check and disprove much of what is said. The younger generations are doing that, and it is hard to imagine these talk show personalities will keep their influence much longer. I would argue that the future is not so bright for these conservative talk-radio darlings. Their demographic is aging. It is primarily the 70-year old, white, Protestant in small towns and suburbia, and that is a shrinking demographic.

The 1960 presidential debate between Vice-President Richard Nixon and Democratic Senator John F. Kennedy was the first to be televised. It was undeniable that television would have a place in shaping the political landscape. Television gave elected officials and candidates a new way to speak directly to millions, face to face. It is interesting to note that voter turnout has declined since 1960, the year of that first debate. (2004 and 2008 were exceptions)

Today, with 24-hour cable news stations, it would seem we have more coverage than ever. However, there is concern that many of these shows are not just reporting news but driving our political discussions into the gutter. The television stations, with all those time slots to fill, have introduced us to analysis by their hosts, the "talking heads" as we call them. These talking heads lean toward one party or the other and have guests on to spin the news in their favor. The use of out of context sound bites are used to influence opinion. Sean Hannity is a multimedia superstar. As host of *The Sean Hannity Show*, his incendiary, political commentary has made him the second-most listened to talk radio host in the U.S. He commands an audience of fourteen million weekly listeners. In addition to his radio broadcasts, he is also a television host on the FOX News Channel and has authored three books. Televised congressional proceedings have politicians engaging in theatrics for the cameras and publicity. Even late-night TV has gone political.

What used to be a source of comedy now is endless political commentary.

In the United States mainstream media can shape public viewpoints. They control the way in which news is presented as well as what news even gets reported. Since they set what the public sees, it is simple for them to subtly push their own agenda. Certain viewpoints are shown by omitting certain details and emphasizing others. This slanting or spinning of information is called media bias. While the information may be factually correct, it gets skewed so that the viewer gets a different impression about the event. It is unfortunate for all of us that the distribution of factual, objective, honest information is so difficult to find in today's mainstream media.

The media has capitalized by playing to our own viewpoints. It is normal for many individuals to judge those with differing views as biased or uninformed. Liberals complain about Sean Hannity (FOX) and conservatives complain about Rachel Maddow (MSNBC). If the hosts do not clearly indicate they are giving their own partisan opinions, their broadcasts can be deceptive. It is becoming increasingly difficult to get information without bias. I have personally flipped back and forth between FOX and MSNBC to try to get a complete picture of events, and difficult is an understatement.

So, what happened to old fashioned news reporting? The answer lies with falling viewership of news programs. Cable news tried to be more entertaining and became less like news and more like non-stop interviews, debating, and opinions, much of which is biased propaganda. It has been reported that all regular TV viewership is declining as we have shifted to streaming services. Netflix and Amazon Prime video are cheaper than cable and have few or no commercials. The commercials on TV have become longer and longer, and Comcast and Direct TV are among the most hated companies in the U.S. Their customer service has been horrendously incompetent.

The problem associated with the formats for news reporting is that many times Americans just cannot tell the difference when opinion is injected. Historically, consumers have expected and become used to the idea that the news reporting is objective. But they seek the outlet that most reinforces their views and accept the hosts comments as factual. An opposing station showcasing a different viewpoint is "biased," or "fake news." So many times, they do not see the reflection of their own bias in the mirror. Time will tell, but in the future the public could move away from these cable outlets to stations such as the BBC or PBS. They may retain some audience, but not so robust as it is today.

Here is a final thought; There was and is a media frenzy around Donald Trump. Love him or hate him, he dominates the news. I expect him to do so even with an election loss in 2020. It is in his nature and personality to be at the forefront, and I can picture him on talk stations as the former President, offering his critique on the events of the day with how he would have done it better. I do not believe he will ride off into the sunset and retire as the distinguished elder statesman. We will see.

Chapter Five: Social Media

"For the first time in human history we have available to us the ability to communicate simultaneously with millions of our fellow men…widening vision of national problems and national events." – Herbert Hoover, 1924

Hoover, of course, was referring to radio. Every time technology improves, our methods of communication change with it.

The whole premise of social media is to grab your attention and not let go. Have you noticed that when you go on the site to look at one thing, it leads you to view another, then another? That's the point, and it can be used as entertainment, or it can be used as a form of political indoctrination by feeding you endless conspiracy theories, misinformation, and hate speech.

Let us call it out for what it is, propaganda. Propaganda is the spreading of ideas or statements that are often false or exaggerated, to garner support for a cause, a political leader, or government. It is not anything new and has been around since the printing press was invented, or likely before.

Social media companies utilize the same technology as video game companies. The concept is called "flow," which is a psychology of keeping you moving from one thing to the next and keeping you on their platform. The motivation is obvious: they earn their money when you stay and view more ads. Your captive attention is worth billions in advertising and subscription revenue. Here's the problem: today, Americans are getting a lot of their news from social media. It is used not only by politicians, but also extremist groups. Many are so ridiculous that one wonders why they are believed, yet the viewer is bombarded with them. QAnon gave us Hillary Clinton and other Democrats running an international child sex-trafficking ring, Robert Mueller secretly working with Trump to expose Democrats, and Angela Merkel is Hitler's granddaughter. Deep state rumors and an international cabal with Queen Elizabeth as a member. Sadly, there are many Americans who believe and have an appetite for this stuff. It defies understanding.

In the 2016 Presidential election, Donald Trump and Hillary Clinton spent eighty-one million dollars on Facebook ads. The use of social media in politics including Twitter, Facebook, and YouTube has dramatically changed the way campaigns are run and how Americans interact with their elected officials. Barack Obama was one of the first politicians to tap into the power of social media. His campaign collected and analyzed data on a large scale, enabling them to coordinate and target their communications. Using social media not only allows politicians to target and have direct contact with voters, it allows them to advertise without paying for advertising. For example, they can put something on YouTube for free and journalists writing about it help to publicize it to a wider audience at no cost. The share function on Twitter and Facebook gets their message out to like-minded voters helping the message to go viral. (going viral means that it spreads quickly to millions)

The beauty for a campaign in these outlets is the analytics and targeting capabilities. Messages can be tailored to voter demographics such as over sixty, or under thirty, male, female, etc. They can also serve as a means of fund raising. Most of us have been on the receiving end of the request for a donation by a certain deadline to compensate for some urgent problem. Smart politicians do nothing without knowing how it plays with the electorate. Twitter and Facebook allow them to gauge the public reaction to issues and controversies immediately, so they can adjust their campaigns accordingly. There is also power for citizens to form groups together on these platforms to leverage influence with their elected officials.

With all the benefits to a campaign or a candidate, there are some downsides. A wrong post or tweet can derail a politician's support, or even cost them their seat, as we have seen on a few occasions. Most campaigns have staffers that scrub the social media accounts of anything unflattering, but there is some risk of negative feedback showing up on a feed.

The advances in media technology continue to impact our everyday life. With regards to government and political information, social media has become an important tool for citizens to gain knowledge, and perhaps to engage in the political process itself. Some believe this can lead to an online town hall format and serve to increase citizen engagement, certainly a positive impact.

The power of social networking sites is in their ability to reach people who may not have had an interest in voting previously, and to excite them over an issue or candidate. For example, a Facebook group known as "Students for Obama" was created after Obama announced his candidacy. In less than one year, it had 62,000 members and chapters at eighty colleges. The take-away from this is that the support for Obama was not being driven by the campaign and was more spontaneous.

It is not all good news. An interesting observation from the inauguration of Brazil's new far-right President, Jair Bolsanaro, had supporters chanting Facebook and WhatsApp cheers, obviously crediting those platforms with his success. They were not wrong. During the campaign there was a massive propaganda campaign funded by an ultra-conservative pro-business group on WhatsApp. They spread false and damaging information about his opponent which spread rapidly leading up to the election. Authoritarians had learned to utilize social media to their advantage.

It is very easy to use social media to inflame public opinion, and if we are completely honest we can admit, it has become a useful tool for authoritarians. Both Russia and China are skilled at manipulating these platforms, and the platforms themselves allow for ease of avoiding censorship. If you place a deluge of false information, conspiracy theories, rumors, and reported "leaks," the fact-checking cannot keep up and the fake stories go viral, taking on a life of their own.

Here is an uncomfortable truth that is sure to alienate Trump supporters. Donald Trump and his allies employ a similar strategy to what was seen in Brazil. He lies; he lies frequently. Right-wing outlets spread the falsehoods, many times with manufactured supporting evidence, to his hardcore supporters who perhaps unwittingly, share and post the lie as factual and truthful information.

Researchers from the University of Oxford conducted a study on social media sharing, and their findings are interesting. Conservatives were more than four times as likely to share fake news on Facebook than liberals. "On Twitter, a network of Trump supporters consumes the largest volume of junk news, and junk news is the largest proportion of news links they share," and, "Extreme hard right Facebook pages – distinct from Republican pages – share more junk news than all the other audiences put together." The point is this; maybe we cannot blame social media companies for what is occurring, but their very platforms enable a politician to abuse it, spread misinformation, and gain an unfair advantage over his opponent. All of this is damaging to our democracy. When the news is deemed as all fake news, citizens may become indifferent, disengaged, cynical, and even hostile to democratic institutions.

There is some more positive information for us as we enter the 2020 election year. PEW research reports in a most recent study that Democrats and Republicans alike, do not place much trust in social media sites. I would add that confidence in government is at an all-time low as well. Obviously, social media has become an important news source for American politics, but an unfortunate reality is that consumers stay in their own polarized news bubble, and only listen to unfiltered and unchallenged reports.

One important thing social media (primarily Facebook) is doing today that changes our political picture is through their use of "dark posts." Bloomberg Businessweek published an article just prior to the last Presidential election about this. They found the Trump campaign utilized what they called "dark operations" to undermine support for

Hillary Clinton. They used non-public posts that can only be seen by followers, and they were designed to depress the African American turnout in Florida and elsewhere. Just like in Brazil, it had an effect. You could never get away with that on a traditional media site.

When we see ads on TV, they are required to note the source, who paid for it, etc. The social media platforms should be required to open themselves for that kind of scrutiny by analysts and the public. Then we could know how much of this is out there, and who is paying for it.

A final note on social media and President Trump: when critiqued about his use of social media, particularly Twitter, as not being presidential; his response was, "Not presidential – it's modern-day presidential."

Chapter Six: Lobbyists

Lobbyist: a person who takes part in an organized attempt to influence legislators.

When we think of lobbyists, most of us tend to believe this is a modern phenomenon, but basic forms of lobbying have been around since the early 1600's. In the 1640's, the British House of Commons allowed the public to appeal to Representatives in the lobby of the legislature building. That practice was carried over from England to America and our forefathers included the right to petition in the First Amendment of our U.S. Constitution.

After the American Revolution, colonists used their new independence to voice their needs and opinions to community leaders and lawmakers. That was an early form of lobbying. By the 1840's, the term lobbying was appearing in newspapers, and Ulysses Grant gave the term popularity when he referred to people who tried to petition him as he enjoyed a cigar in the lobby of the Willard Hotel as lobbyists.

Modern-day lobbying is now a formal, regulated practice that provides an influential way for voices and opinions to be heard on both the state and national level. Members of the lobbying industry represent clients – corporations, trade groups, and nonprofits to advocate on their behalf. The relationship is complicated because lobbyists pursue relationships with lawmakers so they can help shape legislation favorable to their clients. Conversely, lobbyists are targeted by lawmakers as sources for campaign funds, which the lobbyists feel obligated to give. Surely, one can see the problem in this.

Politicians can get extraordinary sums of money from these special interest groups. In return, they create laws favorable to these groups, even when it may hurt voters. Lobbyists can use their ability to bundle together big contributions from friends and colleagues and deliver even larger sums to politicians. This effectively turns lobbyists into major fundraisers, and politicians have an incentive to keep them happy with their political favors. Once again, the tail is wagging the dog.

Another problem with this whole system is the revolving door, where politicians move into high-paying lobbying jobs where they are paid to influence their former colleagues. We all know this is not the best situation, yet it is allowed and happens frequently.

Elections are flooded with money from everywhere. Some of these donations are difficult, if not impossible to track. Money gets funneled through groups with secret donors, who in turn make unlimited contributions to super PACS. They can spend generously by buying massive airtime to influence an election and defeat a candidate. Running political campaigns is expensive, and most Americans could never afford to make major donations. That leaves politicians dependent on these special interest donors. The fact is that whether Americans are for or against an idea really has little impact on Congress. What has the influence is money. Here are ten-year statistics on spending to influence our government, by industry.

- Pharmaceutical $2.16 Billion
- Energy $2.93 Billion
- Defense $1.26 Billion
- Finance $4.29 Billion
- Agribusiness $1.21 Billion
- Communications $3.50 Billion

Did you notice the amount spent to lobby for defense spending? I must admit, it left me surprised that it was so much lower than the others, but I conclude it is much easier to get Congress to spend on defense, as is evidenced by their increasing budgets passed with bipartisan support. They are spending billions to influence our government, and we give them trillions in return. They have received a return of 750 times their investment. Moneyed interests get what they want, and the rest of us pay the price. It is a cycle of legalized corruption.

Did you know that the candidate with the most money wins the election 91% of the time? That is why politicians spend up to 70% of their time fundraising instead of governing.

Many years ago, a business colleague of mine confided a story to me that has stuck with me for many years. Through his family political connections, he was able to obtain a job as a driver/chauffeur for a candidate running for governor. He was young, impressionable, and naïve. He told me that paper bags and briefcases filled with cash were given to them often on the campaign trail. It did not take him long to realize that many of the staffers were helping themselves to a few hundred here and there. Soon, he was doing it too. He joked that he did not want to ever win an election, he just wanted to run because there was big money in being a candidate.

We all have a right to make our voices heard. I am appalled at our Supreme Court rulings that tell us money is a protected form of speech. Cases like *Citizens United* opened the door for unlimited "dark money" campaign spending. This infuriates me and it should you too. If you do not have the cash, you will probably be ignored. The playing field could not be any more uneven.

Lobbying has been described as bribery in a suit. Bribery, of course, is illegal. Lobbying is not. The distinction between these two in the U.S. is a bit fuzzy. There have been some large bribery scandals involving some familiar names. Kellogg, Brown & Root (now KBR, Inc.) was part of Halliburton. You may know the name from large U.S. military contracts. They were convicted of paying hundreds of millions of dollars to Nigerian officials to secure a natural gas plant construction project. There are scores of others.

Bribery is the first step of subversion of the economic system. Over time, it erodes the economic foundation of the country and fills the public with feelings of hopelessness and cynicism. All too often, the border between lobbying and bribery is blurred. Wouldn't it be considered a form of bribery to offer a politician a lucrative job as a lobbyist? Con men, swindlers, and cheaters pay bribes. Executives in suits hire lobbyists because they get better, longer lasting results, and rarely land in jail. I think most Americans would agree that a bribe is a bribe.

I think we all understand that Congress is in no rush to reform itself. Do you remember the lobbyist Jack Abramoff? In 2005 he was arrested, and the worst of lobbying excesses were exposed. He openly hosted lawmakers on golf trips to Scotland, exotic dinners, and gave lavish campaign contributions. He opened the door for lobbyists to write their own legislation. As a result, House Majority Leader Tom DeLay (R-Texas) resigned, and Ohio Representative Bob Ney went to prison. That led to Democrats retaking both chambers, and promising voters to change the "culture of corruption."

That promise led to enactment of the Honest Leadership and Open Government Act of 2007. Senator Harry Reid said, "This legislation will slow the revolving door that shuffles lawmakers and top staff between federal jobs and the private sector," and Senator Susan Collins assured the bill would restore the public's trust. Quite the opposite, I am afraid, is true.

The bill did not stop the revolving door; what it did instead is create an entire new group of professional influencers that are out of the public eye and unaccountable. The work-around comes in the form of policy advisers, strategic consultants, trade association CEO's, corporate government relations executives, affiliates of research institutes that are agenda-driven, and leaders of political action committees, etc. More former lawmakers than ever are influencing policy, just not necessarily as registered lobbyists. The rules of the law were so weak, with so many loopholes, that criminal penalties have never even been tried. What they did was pass a bill that changed nothing. Does this pass your internal smell test? The law was deliberately watered down by lawmakers that were concerned about their own future job prospects.

Oh, and in case you are curious, the DOJ ultimately dropped charges against Tom DeLay, and he was acquitted in Texas on charges there. Today, he is a healthcare lobbyist, an author, and has appeared on the TV show, *Dancing with the Stars*.

It seems we are all dancing too. For us, it is the limbo; continuously lowering the bar on a race to the bottom.

So how do we fix this and get rid of this political bribery? The five steps below will accomplish this.

1. Make it illegal for politicians to take money from lobbyists.
2. Ban lobbyists from "bundling" contributions.
3. Close the revolving door. Ban paid lobbying jobs for several years.
4. Prevent fundraising during working hours.
5. Stop donors from hiding behind secret money groups, and immediately disclose political money online.

All these steps are in suggested legislation by the group, represent.us. They are calling it *The American Anti-Corruption Act.*

It is common sense to many of us, but we know Congress has little appetite for regulating itself. It will take a coordinated effort (lobbying), with a lot of public pressure to get this done.

Chapter Seven: Term Limits

Since America's founding in 1776, term limits have been a hotly debated issue in U.S. politics. Yet, even from the very beginning the power of term limits to guard against oligarchy and preserve representative government was well understood.

"I apprehend that the total abandonment of the principle of rotation in the offices of president and senator will end in abuse." – Thomas Jefferson

"After a time, civil servants tend to become no longer servants and no longer civil." – Winston Churchill

"Term limits would cure both senility and seniority-both terrible legislative diseases." – Harry Truman

And one more final quote from the infamous lobbyist, Jack Abramoff: *"As a lobbyist, I was completely against term limits, and I know a lot of people are against term limits, and I was one of the leaders, because why? As a lobbyist, once you buy a congressional office, you don't have to re-buy that office in six years, right?"*

The fears of our framers, today, have been realized. The rise of career politicians has removed the power from "We, The People" and transferred it to Congress.

One of the main arguments in favor of term limits is that the framers did not expect government to be run by professional politicians. This implies that there is some sort of evil in being a professional politician, and they wanted to guard against it. There is also an argument against imposing term limitations, and the real history of our founders does conflict with the notion of having limits.

Consider this, Thomas Jefferson was a professional politician by any definition. He served for over forty years combined in the Congress, the Virginia legislature, Governor of Virginia, U.S. Secretary of State, Vice-President, and finally as President. James Madison was also a career politician. Most of the founders were long-term officeholders. Connecticut's Roger Sherman, a signer of the Declaration of Independence and a drafter of the U.S. Constitution held office from 1769 until his death. He served seven consecutive terms in the Continental Congress, a term in the U.S. House of Representatives, and was in the U.S. Senate when he died. Under a term limits rule, these men could not have served so long. There are many other notables in our history that we may not have seen if there were term limitations. Opponents of term limits argue that our founders were more concerned that we have the most capable people running our government, that experience matters, and term limits could get in the way of that.

"Nothing renders government more unstable than a frequent change of the persons that administer it." – Roger Sherman, 1788

Even though there is widespread support (75% or more of the public) for limitations, there are a few downsides that should be considered.

Does it take power away from voters? If the voters really want someone, and that person is barred from being on the ballot, then you are restricting voter choice.

Policymaking and crafting legislative proposals, is a learned skill. Sometimes societal issues are complex things, without simple answers, and the public may not be best served by inexperienced lawmakers. It takes a long time to learn and master all the various rules and procedures of Congress, to form coalitions and alliances to get things done, and term limits forces the seasoned members out the door.

Another possible problem is members who know their time is limited may lack incentive to gain policy expertise. Fewer lawmakers with experience could result in even more influence by special interest groups rushing in to fill the information void for the inexperienced legislator.

Term limits could force the best employees out of a job. Doesn't it make more sense to keep them to utilize their skills and talent? It seems like a bad return on investment.

The big issue of course for many of us is the corruption and the revolving door of the lobbying industry. As mentioned previously, instead of curtailing influence, the opposite could occur as newbie lawmakers turn to special interests for information on a topic or industry. Since limits have never existed on the federal level, political scientists have studied state and foreign governments to judge the effects. What their studies find is that term limits have, unfortunately, served to exacerbate corruption.

Based upon these arguments, one might conclude that the best way to remove an ineffective or unresponsive member of Congress is with our current method: elections.

Term limits are opposed primarily by elected officials and the special-interest groups that depend on them. It is obvious why a member of Congress would not view term limitations favorably. They have a starting salary of $174,000 and up to 230 days off. (If you do the math, that is $1,289 per day worked)

There are other perks that most of us could not imagine. The senate dining room is a first-class, elite restaurant that the rest of us probably could not afford. They fly first-class and have free reserved parking at both Regan and Dulles airports. They are allowed $40,000 just for office furnishings. Have you heard of the "franking privilege?" It allows them to spend $50,000 for mass mailings, and that gives an advantage to any incumbent. Their annual expense accounts range from $1.2 million to as high as $4 million dollars. That is per member. It is supposed to cover staff salaries, food, and travel expenses. I can tell you as the CEO of a medium-sized company, never did I have such a perk.

Most of us know of their top-tier healthcare, but they also have a top-tier "wellness center" with an indoor tennis court, and other country-club amenities. By the way, the Senate Hair Care Services is a longstanding, taxpayer-subsidized barber shop and salon.

Wait, there is more. Maybe you did not know this one; they have a private subway, so they don't have to walk outside to get to their offices. You may have heard that they receive compensation for life, and that is not exactly true. But depending on age and length of service they could receive up to 80% of pay in their pension program.

Who would want to give all of that up?

The problem, as it exists today, is the best and brightest tend to not run since it is nearly impossible to defeat an incumbent. They must wait for the incumbent to retire, die, or go to prison. In 2017, Senate Majority Leader Mitch McConnell said, "We have term limits. They're called elections." I would add, "but they're not fair elections." If we open the process by removing the barriers to entry, more candidates will run, and the public will get the kind of democracy it wants and deserves.

While we are on the subject, one area that has been debated is the lifetime appointment to the

Supreme Court. Justice Neil Gorsuch said that the framers of our constitution did not want "nine old people in Washington sitting in robes telling everybody else how to live." Yet, that is what we have.

We have seen Justices stay on way past their prime, and we have seen the contentious political confirmation hearings. The fact is, these are the people making the decisions for us, and perhaps it would make sense for either a term limit or mandatory retirement age.

In the past, we have had politicians who had no business occupying a seat in the Senate or the House. The most obvious example was Senator Strom Thurmond (R-SC). He served forty-seven years until 2003, the year he died. He was 100. He was so frail and under sedation, he needed assistance standing up from his chair. Senator Dianne Feinstein (D-CA) is 87. There are many others well into their eighties still serving. I salute them for their service, but there must be a point in time where we usher in the fresh blood, fresh ideas, and vigor of the next generation. Do we want our highest court judges and congressional representatives making crucial decisions when they are past their prime?

Common sense dictates the need for changes to our current system. We need term limits for all government representatives. We need a cutoff age of 80 for the Supreme Court, and Presidential candidates need to be under 80 during their term. I do not say this to be cruel, just sensible. I don't think it matters how smart or experienced you are. Even if you are in great shape at 80, you have no business being President, a Supreme Court Justice, or a member of Congress.

Chapter Eight: Politicians

Why would anyone want to enter the harsh world of politics? In the previous chapters, we covered their financial rewards and perks. But is that the only motivation? Perhaps some feel the allure of power. It has been said that politics presents to man two irresistible allures – power and corruption.

Political power is the ability to control the behavior of people through the passage, approval, and implementation of laws and regulations. Simply put, those who hold political power control how the masses live their lives. This power is not necessarily bad, because we need it for the well-being of society. Without it, there would be no laws and society would disintegrate.

If you were to ask a political leader or candidate if they are interested in power, they would, of course, deny it. You would likely hear comments such as "sharing their leadership qualities," or taking the "important responsibility to lead," maybe even "they are doing God's work." None will admit to being power hungry. Yet, it is human nature to try and become the alpha male, just like in the animal kingdom. Political candidates will say they are interested in healthcare or fiscal responsibility, but never will you hear "I love power."

To fully understand the drive to attain power, first we should recognize that these are not "normal" people. They tend to show different behaviors, good or bad, that are more inherent in those climbing to the top. Fortune favors the bold. Perhaps if we look closely at some politicians of the past and present, we can find what drove them to politics.

Donald Trump: Why would a billionaire real estate mogul and reality television personality want to enter politics? In his 1987 book, *The Art of the Deal*, he described how he successfully makes business deals. "I don't do it for the money. I've got enough, much more than I'll ever need. I do it to do it. Deals are my art form." You need a healthy-sized ego to be in politics, and perhaps a degree of narcissism. Some would say in Trump's case, it is ego and narcissism run amok.

Ray Nagin: Nagin was the Mayor of New Orleans who profited from the 2005 Hurricane Katrina disaster. He used the disaster to profit from millions of dollars in no-bid contracts, and steered redevelopment business to a company he owned with his sons. He received a ten-year prison sentence.

The Keating Five: Have you heard of the Keating Five? Charles Keating's Lincoln Savings and Loan in California collapsed in 1989 and left many investors penniless. How he got away with it for so long was through generous donations to five politicians who intervened with regulators on his behalf. They were Alan Cranston (D-CA), Dennis DeConcini (D-AZ), Donald Riegle (D-MI), John Glenn (D-OH), and John McCain (R-AZ). Senator Cranston received a "formal reprimand," while Senators DeConcini and Reigle were criticized for "acting improperly." Senators Glenn and McCain were cleared of wrongdoing, but "formally criticized" for poor judgement. Would you agree that most of that sounds like not much happened to them?

Randy "Duke" Cunningham (R-CA): Cunningham used his status as a member of the House Defense Appropriations Subcommittee to help with lucrative government contracts for his defense contractor buddies. His home was purchased for twice the market value, and he lived rent-free on a yacht. Other bribes were cash payments and a Rolls Royce. He received an eight-year prison sentence.

Edwin Edwards: Former Louisiana Governor Edwards was charged in corruption cases twenty-four times and won every single time. The twenty-fifth proved to be the final straw, where his scheme to extort millions for state casino licenses landed him eight years in prison.

There are so many of these that one could fill an entire book just writing about the various cases and types of corruption. President Warren Harding was implicated in 1921 in the "Teapot Dome Scandal," and one of his cabinet members went to prison. And of course, arguably the most infamous of all, President Richard Nixon and the Watergate Scandal, causing him to resign the presidency.

So, should we believe then, that all politicians are pathological liars, thieves, and sexual predators? Perhaps we should.

Consider this: Several years ago, Katie Couric did a story regarding political retirements. What was shocking (or maybe not) in her story was even the political thieves, liars, and crooks who were caught and sent to prison continued to receive their six-figure retirement income from us generous taxpayers, while they were behind bars. Outrageous? You bet it is! By the way, they also received cost of living increases, but those of you on fixed social security or disability income did not.

Politicians have helped create a political atmosphere wherein many people just do not vote, out of frustration that it doesn't make any difference.

There is an old joke that goes "99% of lawyers have given the other 1% a bad name." The Bible has this verse, Romans, CH.1, v. 22 – "claiming to be wise, they become fools."

Today, most politicians seem to be followers of Machiavelli's beliefs. Niccolò Machiavelli was an Italian diplomat, known for his political treatise, *The Prince,* written in 1513. His work encourages "the end justifies the means" behavior. In his work, he claimed that Princes should use force and fraud to achieve political objectives, and that it was right to do so. I am not so sure that would pass the smell test today.

"There is no distinctly native American criminal class except Congress." – Mark Twain

So, what are "We, The People" to do? The greed and ambition of our leaders has spiraled out of control for so long, it seems impossible to reel it in. There is no silver bullet for fighting corruption, but there are some ways that might start to break the cycle.

Fighting from the top down probably works no better than trickle-down economics. We need an end-run around Congress because they are incapable of policing themselves. It starts with local and statewide elections and trickles up. Candidates who win on anti-corruption campaigns have a built-in incentive to champion for those similar laws in Washington, D.C. Remember, the biggest changes in America have almost always started at the state and local levels.

"If we elect the same corrupt politicians every time, that's a very clear message that we don't want a change." – Sukant Ratnakar

Chapter Nine: Socialism

Since I believe in certain government-provided programs such as social security, universal basic income, a job guarantee plan, and Medicare for all, the editors felt it would be prudent to add a chapter addressing my views about socialism. So here are my views on the matter.

So, what exactly do we mean when we say socialism? It seems to mean different things to many people. Why do some say it means we will become communists? There is a lot of fear and misunderstanding surrounding it, so maybe we should dig a little deeper.

Both socialism and communism are just economic philosophies that advocate public rather than private ownership of the production of goods. Both philosophies aim to correct problems from a capitalist system, such as worker exploitation and the ever-widening gap between rich and poor. Socialism and communism are similar at their base, but there are notable differences.

We first saw socialism emerge during the Industrial Revolution when workers grew increasingly poor, while industrialists achieved massive wealth. Then along came Karl Marx, with his *The Communist Manifesto*, in which he criticized socialism as unrealistic, and utopian dreaming. Some Marxists believe socialism is the necessary first step toward communism, which gives us the confusion we see today. I believe that is where the fear originates; that if we get on that slippery slope of socialism, we are somehow doomed to become communists.

I say not so fast. Under socialism, individuals can still own property. It is a less rigid system with a more flexible ideology. Change and reform come through the democratic process in place, not an overthrow of the government. A socialist economic system rewards individual effort and innovation, and easily co-exists with a free-market capitalist economy.

But there are some dangers. What is democratic socialism, and how is it supposed to be different? When being interviewed by Stephen Colbert, the popular freshman Congresswoman Alexandria Ocasio-Cortez said "what that means to me is health care as a human right. It means that every child, no matter where you are born, should have access to a college or trade school education if they so choose it." Senator Bernie Sanders says "in the wealthiest country in the history of the world, economic rights are human rights. That is what I mean by democratic socialism." What is the danger? To implement the economic rights suggested by Ocasio-Cortez and Sanders, Medicare for all abolishes private insurance and gives government control of the health care industry. Allegedly, college for all pushes private schools to take more federal money, and over time there would be little difference between a public or private school.

These are good points. Perhaps there is a compromise. Under Medicare, there are numerous insurance companies providing the benefit through their Medicare Advantage Plans. The industry seems to be doing just fine, and what we are really talking about is who pays. They bill the government just like regular Medicare, but they are getting the Medicare monthly premium for each enrollee. They also get an opportunity to offer upgrades for additional premiums to their members. As for education, who can argue against the fact that it has become unaffordable? I believe we have encouraged our young people to take on massive debt for their education and have not put enough emphasis on learning skilled trades. Surely, there are compromises here as well.

"Students who acquire large debts putting themselves through school are unlikely to think about changing society. When you trap people in a system of debt, they can't afford the time to think." *– Noam Chomsky*

Democratic Socialism was the compact between government, business, and citizenry that built all of America's infrastructure between 1930 and 1980.

Your elementary through high school, fire department, police department, library, roads, street lights, water treatment, dams, levees, airports, highway system, Army, Navy, Air Force, Marines, Post Office, garbage, court house, FDA, OSHA, CDC, snow plows, street sweepers, electrical grid – all of that was our tax dollars used by the government to contract businesses to hire Americans to build our country into a powerhouse.

Your American Dream was built on Democratic Socialism. Unfettered capitalism destroyed it. America was not always like this.

There is a fear that democratic socialism will lead us to tyranny. Democracy was originally majority rule, but the fear is a tyranny of the majority. Our

U.S. Constitution was designed to protect against this. Voting is our safeguard, but only for as long as the majority cannot vote away our rights. There is always the underlying concern of a demagogue seizing power and proclaiming themselves to be implementing "the will of the people." Democratic socialists claim they will avoid the failures from the past, and critics will point to Venezuela for their most recent example of a country that went from democratically elected, to socialism, and now (possibly) a dictatorship.

What about Venezuela?

Venezuela used to be the wealthiest country in South America. Until recently, almost all of Venezuela's population, primarily urban and educated, had access to clean drinking water, sanitation facilities, and electricity. They have the largest fossil-fuel reserves in the world and were an affluent country. Today, they have a shrinking economy and out of control inflation. There is poverty, and violent protests have ensued. They are in economic collapse.

What went wrong? Before we hasten to blame socialism itself, we should observe the mistakes from the leadership over the years.

It is no secret that Venezuela has long been dependent on oil revenue. Since 1922 when oil was discovered in the Maracaibo basin of western Venezuela, their fortunes have been tied together. The Dictator at that time, Juan Vincente Gómez, allowed foreign oil companies into the country, and by 1928 Venezuela had become the world's second-biggest petroleum exporter.

The influx of oil money enriched the regime, and in 1943 a law was passed forcing foreign oil companies to share half of their profits. By 1958, the dictatorial style of government was overthrown, and a president was elected. Rómulo Betancourt became President and many people regard him as the father of Venezuelan democracy. At the time of the election, all political parties agreed to abide by the results in the Puntofijio Pact, which guaranteed each of them their piece of the pie, of government ministries, jobs, and contracts. It also kept the oil revenue in the hands of government.

In 1973, the OPEC embargo against the United States and others caused the price of oil to quadruple. Venezuela became the beneficiary of that action and billions flowed into their treasury. Two years later a law was enacted nationalizing the oil industry, and a state-owned oil company was created.

In the late 1980's oil prices plummeted, and the government struggled under the weight of foreign debt. Eventually, they were forced to accept a bailout from the IMF (International Monetary Fund) and to impose austerity measures that resulted in higher prices for consumer goods. These caused protests and violent demonstrations, which led to a nationwide curfew and suspension of civil liberties.

In 1998, the populist leader Hugo Chávez was elected President. Over the next fifteen years he conducted a massive social spending spree by redirecting oil profits to programs that addressed social inequality. His programs achieved the goal of reducing poverty, but at the same time increased the dependence on oil revenue. Chávez wanted to diversify the economy, but his strategy was expensive. He wanted to increase Venezuelan influence by selling oil at discounted prices to other countries. Unfortunately, he neglected to put money into maintaining oil facilities and production declined. When oil revenue declines, the Venezuelan economy declines with it.

After Chávez died of cancer, his hand-picked successor Nicolás Maduro took over, and has been consolidating his power ever since.

This is where Venezuela is today. Expropriations, weak public-sector institutions, nationalizations, overregulation, soaring crime rates, corruption, and a thoroughly politicized judiciary have greatly undermined real property rights. The government's economic policies, particularly currency and price controls, have greatly increased black-market activity, and collusion between public officials and organized crime networks is rampant. We can blame it all on socialism, or we can blame mismanagement and corruption.

Venezuela's mistake lies in their failure to become and maintain a mixed economy; an economy that utilizes some capitalist and some socialist principles. The government can control some aspects, but private individuals and corporations control others. A mixed economy relies on the law of supply and demand to determine production and prices.

I believe it may be too difficult to have a quest for a purely socialist, or for that matter, a purely capitalist society. Even the United States, considered one of the most successful capitalist economies in the world, currently has many socialist-inspired programs to help those in need. For now, it seems that a mixed economy, featuring both socialist and capitalist elements, is more realistic.

And since we are talking about Venezuela: The mercenaries who had the dumb idea to try to invade Venezuela remind me of some of the American people. The mindset of these warrior, Rambo wannabes and the delusions of their collective badassery are kind of pathetic. Some of our gun-toting civilians and gun rights advocates appear to imagine themselves as the last line of defense against a corrupt government. It is likely that these gun owners would have about as much success against government police or military as the Venezuelan invaders. Maybe we have watched too many movies where Joe Average guy saves the world. Think about it: middle-aged, overweight, poorly trained, or untrained, disorganized people going against an organized, equipped, well-trained army. For their trouble, these men have been sentenced to twenty years in a Venezuelan prison.

<u>Conclusion</u>

America is an exceptional country, and Americans are an exceptional people. Certainly, we all have our flaws and have equally made our share of mistakes. The title of this book makes the point. Our opinions change and the song lyrics, at least to me, reflect on those changes. Sometimes it is the left foot or hand; sometimes it is the right foot or hand; and sometimes it is our whole self, shaking about. If you are anything like me, your views change over time. I know mine have and probably will again.

But, in spite of our differences; even with all the vitriol on social media or the rage spewing from talk-radio and TV; I believe we are a kind and generous people and that culture of good has been ingrained in us. It is in our nature.

I choose to believe that our great nation will weather our current political storm and emerge as that "beacon of light" that Ronald Reagan spoke of years ago. I also believe we can provide social safety nets without endangering our democracy or our economy. We have an ability to make this great American experiment soar ever higher. Our country and our politics have changed and evolved many times, just as our personal views do. We will do it again because we must.

I don't think I can be convinced, that in this wealthy nation of ours, we can't provide a certain level of social services to truly benefit the lives of the people. The system can never be perfect; it will always have flaws. I would never wish for our government to turn communist, nor do I want it to be fascist or fully socialist. What I prefer to see are a few social programs in place; social security for the elderly firmly in place and expanded, universal healthcare, and some form of universal basic income. With these in place, the American people could truly prosper. I don't believe a few benevolent programs mean we are destroying the country. At the very least, we should begin honest conversations about changing the direction of this country. Our current system of funding continuous wars and feeding money into an ever-growing military-industrial complex is misguided. Our infrastructure is crumbling around us and our great middle-class is rapidly disappearing. We need change, and we need it soon.

By the way, the following is a short list of some people that were socialist or communist. Some of the American heroes on this list may surprise you.

Martin Luther King, Albert Einstein, Nelson Mandela, Frida Kahlo, Tupac Shakur, Mark Twain, Malcom X, Oscar Wilde, Bertrand Russell, Helen Keller, Pablo Picasso, George Orwell, Shia LaBeouf, John Lennon, and Woody Guthrie.

Socialism and communism are not dirty words. Some of the most brilliant minds of our history were socialists and communists. Embrace it.

"To accept your country without betraying it, you must love it for that which shows what it might become. America – this monument to the genius of ordinary men and women, this place where hope becomes capacity, this long halting turn of 'no' into the 'yes' – needs citizens who love it enough to re-imagine and re-make it." – Cornel West

www.ingramcontent.com/pod-product-compliance
Lightning Source LLC
Chambersburg PA
CBHW070815240726
48654CB00007B/353